SELECTED POEMS

PIERRE REVERDY

Selected Poems

KENNETH REXROTH

A NEW DIRECTIONS BOOK

Published by arrangement with Editions Gallimard, Paris, and Mercure de France, Paris. The poems in this selection are from the French volumes *Plupart du temps* (Gallimard) and *Main d'oeuvre* (Mercure). Eight of the translations first appeared in *New Directions 15* anthology.

The Juan Gris illustrations are from *Denise* by Raymond Radiguet, Kahnweiler, Paris, 1926; courtesy of Department of Printing and Graphic Arts, Houghton Library, Harvard University.

Designed by Roderick D. Stinehour and printed
at The Stinehour Press, Lunenburg, Vermont.

New Directions Books are published for James Laughlin
by New Directions Publishing Corporation,
333 Sixth Avenue, New York 10014

INTRODUCTION

THE POETS associated with Cubism are Guillaume Apolli-
naire, Blaise Cendrars, Jean Cocteau, Max Jacob, André Salmon
and Pierre Reverdy. As the years have passed and *cette belle
époque* recedes into perspective, for us today, Pierre Reverdy
stands out from his fellows as the most profound and most con-
trolled artist. This is part of a general revaluation which has
taken place as the latter half of the century has come to judge
the first half. So Robert Desnos has risen above his Surrealist
colleagues and competitors. So independents like Supervielle,
Milosz and Léon-Paul Fargue are more appreciated today than
they were in their lifetimes. Just as Francis Jammes has almost
overwhelmed the poetic reputations of the beginning of the
century and the once world-famous Verhaeren is hardly read at
all, so from the Fantaisistes, the poets of *Le Divan*, Toulet and
Francis Carco almost alone survive. Although time has seldom
worked so quickly, I am more or less confident that those re-
valuations will stand. Certainly Pierre Reverdy's present posi-
tion should be secure. International literary taste has learned
the idiom, the syntax that was so new and strange in 1912.
Fortuitous novelty has fallen away and this has enabled com-
prehension and judgment. Neither Reverdy nor Tristan Tzara
can shock anybody any more. And so those values once masked
by shock enter into the judgment of a later generation.

Juan Gris was Pierre Reverdy's favorite illustrator, as he in
turn was the painter's favorite poet. No one today would deny

that they share the distinction of being the most Cubist of the Cubists. This is apparent to all in Juan Gris. But what is Cubism in poetry? It is the conscious, deliberate dissociation and recombination of elements into a new artistic entity made self-sufficient by its rigorous architecture. This is quite different from the free association of the Surrealists and the combination of unconscious utterance and political nihilism of Dada.

When I was a young lad I thought that literary Cubism was the future of American poetry. Only Walter Conrad Arensberg in his last poems, Gertrude Stein in *Tender Buttons* and a very few other pieces, much of the work of the young Yvor Winters and others of his generation of Chicago Modernists, Laura Riding's best work and my own poems later collected in *The Art of Worldly Wisdom* could be said to show the deliberate practice of the principles of creative construction which guided Juan Gris or Pierre Reverdy. It is necessary to make a sharp distinction between this kind of verse and the Apollinairian technique of *The Waste Land*, *The Cantos*, *Paterson*, Zukofsky's *A*, J. G. MacLeod's *Ecliptic*, Lowenfels' *Some Deaths*, the youthful work of Sam Beckett and Nancy Cunard and, the last of all, David Jones's *Anathemata*.

In poems such as these, as in Apollinaire's "Zone," the elements, the primary data of the poetic construction, are narrative or at least informative wholes. In verse such as Reverdy's, they are simple, sensory, emotional or primary informative objects capable of little or no further reduction. Eliot works in *The Waste Land* with fragmented and recombined arguments; Pierre Reverdy with dismembered propositions from which subject, operator and object have been wrenched free and restructured into an invisible or subliminal discourse which owes its cogency to its own strict, complex and secret logic.

Poetry such as this attempts not just a new syntax of the word. Its revolution is aimed at the syntax of the mind itself. Its restructuring of experience is purposive, not dreamlike, and hence it possesses an uncanniness fundamentally different in kind from the most haunted utterances of the Surrealist or Symbolist unconscious. Contrary to what we are taught, it appears first in the ultimate expressions of Neo-Symbolism in Mallarmé, in his curious still lifes like "Autre Éventail," in occult dramatic molecules like "Petit Air," and, of course, above all in his hieratic metaphysical ritual, *Un Coup de dés*. It is in this tremendously ambitious poem in fact that all the virtues and the faults of the style, whether practiced by Reverdy, Laura Riding or myself, can be found.

These faults, as well as those virtues which he decided were in fact faults, led Yvor Winters to condemn all verse of this kind as the deliberate courting of madness. What he objected to in essence was the seeking of glamour, that effulgence which St. Thomas called the stigmata of a true work of art, as an end in itself. What James Joyce translates "wholeness, harmony and radiance" are qualities not only of all works of art but they are often sought deliberately. Paul Valéry's objectives are the same as Reverdy's but he presents them in a syntactical context that can be negotiated throughout general experience.

When the ordinary materials of poetry are broken up, recombined in structures radically different from those we assume to be the result of causal, or of what we have come to accept as logical sequence, and then an abnormally focused attention is invited to their apprehension, they are given an intense significance, closed within the structure of the work of art, and are not negotiable in ordinary contexts of occasion. So isolated and illuminated, they seem to assume an unanalyzable transcendental claim. Accompanying, as it were garbing, this insistent transcendence are sometimes certain projected physical responses induced or transmitted in the person undergoing the poetic experience, whether poet or reader. Vertigo, rapture, transport, crystalline and plangent sounds, shattered and refracted light, indefinite depths, weightlessness, piercing odors and tastes, and synthesizing these sensations and affects, an all-consuming clarity. These are the phenomena that often attend what theologians call natural mysticism. They can be found especially in the poetry of St. Mechtild of Magdeburg and St. Hildegarde of Bingen, great favorites of the psychologists who have written on this subject, but they are equally prominent in the poetry of Sappho or Henry Vaughan or the prose of Jacob Boehme, as well as in many modern poets. They have often been equated with the idioretinal and vasomotor disturbances caused by drugs, migraine, or other dissociations of personality, or *petit-mal* epilepsy. At the present moment the quest of such experiences by way of hallucinogenic drugs is immensely fashionable.

I think what Winters meant was that intense hyperesthesia of this type, when it occurs in modern poetry without the motivation of religious belief, is pathological in its most advanced forms and sentimental in its less extreme ones. It is true of course that any work of art that coerces the reader or spectator into intense emotional response for which there is no adequate warrant or motive is by definition sentimental, but I do not think that this is exactly what happens in poetry like that of Reverdy, Mallarmé or Valéry. The putative justifications given by Valéry for the extremities to which he pushes his quest for effulgence are really sops to the reader. His seemingly ordinary informative syntax masks only slightly the same unanalyzable transcendental claim.

We still know almost nothing about how the mind works in states of rapture nor why the disjunction, the ecstasis, of self and experience should produce a whole range of peculiar nervous responses, sometimes quite conscious as in St. Hildegarde, sometimes almost certainly subliminal as in Reverdy or the early poems of Yvor Winters. I am inclined to believe that the persistence of this vocabulary among visionary poets is not a defect but a novitiate. Until rapture becomes an accepted habit, a trained method of apprehending reality, an accustomed instrument, the epiphenomena that accompany its onset will seem unduly important. Since only the intimations of rapture are all that most people are ever aware of, Henry Vaughan's ring of endless light will always serve as an adequate symbol of eternity. Kerkele saw the same idioretinal vision as a very finite ring of carbohydrates.

We are dealing with a self-induced, or naturally and mysteriously come-by, creative state from which two of the most fundamental human activities diverge, the aesthetic and the mystic act. The creative matrix is the same in both, and it is that state of being that is most peculiarly and characteristically human, as the resulting aesthetic or mystic experience is the purest form of human act. There is a great deal of overlapping, today especially, when art is all the religion most people have and when they demand of it experiences that few people of the past demanded even of religion. But a painting by Juan Gris or a poem by Pierre Reverdy is self-evidently not a moment of illumination in the life of St. Teresa of Avila nor even her description of it. It is the difference between centripetal and centrifugal. A visionary poem is not a vision. The religious experience is necessitated and ultimate. The poet may have had such an experience in writing the poem, although probably only to a limited degree, or he would not have had the need to write the poem. But there is nothing necessitated about the poem. We can take it or leave it alone, and any ultimates we find in it we must first bring to it ourselves.

History accustoms the public for poetry, as experience accustoms the poet, to this idiom of radiance. Returned to today, *Un Coup de dés*, or the poems of Reverdy or Laura Riding seem negotiable enough and the similar poems of Yvor Winters seem only passionate love poems or rather simple philosophic apothemes. Reverdy, in fact, in most of his poems is hardly a mystic poet. He simply uses a method which he has learned from his more ambitious poems. It is ambitious enough. He seeks, as all the Cubists did, to present the spectator with a little organism that will take up all experience brought to it, digest it, reorganize it and return it as the aesthetic experience unadulterated. All works of art do this. Artists like Reverdy or Juan Gris sought to do it with a minimum of interference. When they were successful their artifacts were peculiarly indestructible. Today, like the paintings of 1910, Reverdy's poems have become precious objects indeed. They have a special appeal now because, although rigorously classical—(I suppose my description of their method could be called a definition of an hypertrophied classicism, which in a sense was precisely what Cubism was)—they are not in the least depersonalized. Quite the contrary—they are rather shameless. So many of the poems are simple gestures laying bare the heart. For this reason Reverdy has influenced personalist poets like Robert Creeley and Gary Snyder and through them whole schools of younger people.

Reverdy was aware of the final deductions to be made from his poetry as a whole and from his poetic experience when in his most illuminated poems he pushed it to its limits. It is not necessary that the poet have any special religious belief, or any at all, but if poetic vision is refined until it is sufficiently piercing and sufficiently tensile, it cuts through the reality it has reorganized to an existential transcendence. In Reverdy's case the consequences were more specific. In 1930 he retired to the Benedictine Abbey of Solesmes and lived there as a lay associate until his death in 1960 with only rare visits to Paris on business trips or to see old friends.

The revolution of the sensibility that began with Baudelaire became in the latter work of Mallarmé a thoroughgoing syntactical revolution in the language because it was realized that the logical structure of the Indo-European languages was an inadequate vehicle for so profound a change in the sensibility. In actual fact, although Apollinaire is usually considered the watershed of modern poetry, no single poem of his represents as thoroughgoing a change in method as Mallarmé's.

The only attack on the language that was as drastic was the Simultaneism of Henri Barzun, the father of the American critic. Unfortunately the quality of Barzun's work leaves much to be desired and his impact was slight. Gertrude Stein and Walter Conrad Arensberg both went further than anyone writing in French, both in their attempts to provide a new syntax of the sensibility and more simply in applying the methods of Analytical Cubism to poetry. Pierre Reverdy is the first important French poet after *Un Coup de dés* to develop the methods of communication explored by Mallarmé.

The syntactical problems and possibilities of a language are peculiar to that language so the poetry of Reverdy makes unusual demands upon the translator. Certain of his devices would be irrelevant if transmitted directly into English. I have tended to avoid his purposive confusions of tense and mood and used mostly the present or the simple past or future. The subjunctive of course is no longer part of American speech and its use would have destroyed the wry colloquialism so characteristic of Reverdy. Similarly I have used the simple English meanings where Reverdy uses slang of some special métier—for instance, show business. We simply do not have such terms for spotlights and one-wheeled bicycles. Again, "one" is not American speech, and sometimes it has been necessary to use more than one pronoun to translate the French "*on*" when Reverdy is talking about "you," "they" and "I" in the same poem. Otherwise I have tried to keep the translation reasonably literal although there is probably a tendency to assimilate Reverdy's language to that of my own Cubist poetry, Gertrude Stein's *Tender Buttons* or Walter Conrad Arensberg's "For Shady Hill."

Of all modern poets in Western European languages Reverdy has certainly been the leading influence on my own work—incomparably more than anyone in English or American—and I have known and loved his work since I first read *Les Épaves du ciel* as a young boy.

KENNETH REXROTH

SELECTED POEMS

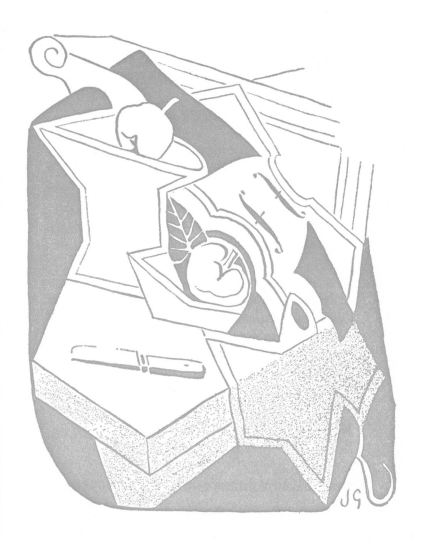

FAUSSE PORTE OU PORTRAIT

Dans la place qui reste là
Entre quatre lignes
          Un carré où le blanc se joue
    La main qui soutenait ta joue
                Lune
    Une figure qui s'allume
          Le profil d'un autre
                    Mais tes yeux
Je suis la lampe qui me guide
Un doigt sur la paupière humide
          Au milieu
      Les larmes roulent dans cet espace
                Entre quatre lignes
                Une glace

SELECTED POEMS

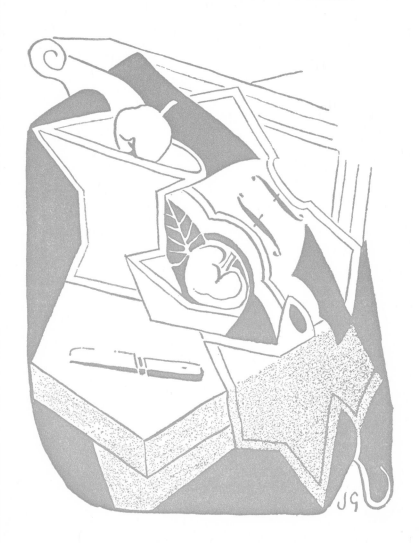

Les yeux à peine ouverts
                    La main sur l'autre rive
Le ciel
            Et tout ce qui arrive
La porte s'inclinait
                Une tête dépasse
Dans le cadre
Et par les volets
On peut regarder à travers
Le soleil prend toute la place
Mais les arbres sont toujours verts
                    Une heure tombe
                    Il fait plus chaud
Et les maisons sont plus petites
Ceux qui passaient allaient moins vite
Et regardaient toujours en haut
                    La lampe à présent nous éclaire
En regardant plus loin
Et nous pouvions voir la lumière
                    Qui venait
Nous étions contents
                    Le soir

Devant l'autre demeure où quelqu'un nous attend

THE SAME NUMBER

The hardly open eyes
        The hand on the other shore
The sky
      And everything that happens there
The leaning door
      A head sticks out
From the frame
And through the shutters
You can see out
The sun fills everything
But the trees are still green
        The falling hour
        It gets warmer
And the houses are smaller
The passersby go less quickly
And always look up
        The lamp shines on us now
Looking far away
We could see the light
        Coming
We were happy
        That evening

At the other house where somebody waits for us

FAUSSE PORTE OU PORTRAIT

Dans la place qui reste là
Entre quatre lignes
           Un carré où le blanc se joue
La main qui soutenait ta joue
              Lune
Une figure qui s'allume
            Le profil d'un autre
                      Mais tes yeux
Je suis la lampe qui me guide
Un doigt sur la paupière humide
              Au milieu
        Les larmes roulent dans cet espace
                  Entre quatre lignes
              Une glace

FALSE DOOR OR PORTRAIT

In the space which lies there
Between four lines
A square where white plays
The hand which held your cheek
Moon
A face which lights up
The profile of another
But your eyes
I am the lamp guiding myself
Finger on damp eyelid
In the midst
The tears flow in this space
Between four lines
Mirror

La couleur que décompose la nuit
La table où ils se sont assis
Le verre en cheminée
      La lampe est un coeur qui se vide
C'est une autre année
     Une nouvelle ride
Y aviez-vous déjà pensé
      La fenêtre déverse un carré bleu
La porte est plus intime
    Une séparation
     Le remords et le crime
Adieu je tombe
Dans l'angle doux des bras qui me reçoivent
Du coin de l'oeil je vois tous ceux qui boivent
     Je n'ose pas bouger
Ils sont assis
      La table est ronde
Et ma mémoire aussi
Je me souviens de tout le monde
Même de ceux qui sont partis

LATE AT NIGHT . . .

The color which night decomposes
The table where they sit
In its glass chimney
        The lamp is a heart emptying itself
It is another year
    A new wrinkle
Would you have thought of it
        The window throws a blue square
The door is more familiar
    A separation
            Remorse and crime
Goodbye I am falling
Gently bending arms take me
Out of the corner of my eye I can see them all drinking
        I don't dare move
They sit there
            The table is round
And so is my memory
I remember everybody
Even those who are gone

La cloche vide
Les oiseaux morts
Dans la maison où tout s'endort
Neuf heures

La terre se tient immobile
On dirait que quelqu'un soupire
Les arbres ont l'air de sourire
L'eau tremble au bout de chaque feuille
Un nuage traverse la nuit

Devant la porte un homme chante

La fenêtre s'ouvre sans bruit

SECRET

The empty bell
The dead birds
In the house where everyone is falling asleep
Nine o'clock

The earth holds itself still
You would say somebody sighed
The trees look like they were smiling
Water trembles at the tip of each leaf
A cloud crosses the night

In front of the door a man is singing

The window opens noiselessly

L<small>E</small> clou est là
    Retient la pente
Le lambeau clair au vent soulevé c'est un souffle
  et celui qui comprend
      Tout le chemin est nu
les pavés les trottoirs la distance le parapet sont
  blancs
          Pas de goutte de pluie
          Pas une feuille d'arbre
          Ni l'ombre d'un habit
              J'attends
              la gare est loin
Pourtant le fleuve coule des quais en remontant
    la terre se dessèche
      tout est nu tout est blanc

Avec le seul mouvement déréglé de l'horloge
      le bruit du train passé
      J'attends

THE DRY TONGUE

THERE is a nail
    Holding up the slope
The bright tatter of twisting wind blows and anyone
    who understands
        The whole road is naked
the pavement the sidewalks the distance the railings are
    white
            Not a drop of rain
            Not a leaf of a tree
            Not the shadow of a garment
                    I wait
                        the station is a long way off
The river still flows as you go up along the embankments
    the earth is dried out
        everything is naked and white

With only the movement of a clock out of order
        the noise of the train passed
           I wait

MIRACLE

Tête penchée
   Cils recourbés
Bouche muette
Les lampes se sont allumées
Il n'y a plus qu'un nom
   Que l'on a oublié
La porte se serait ouverte
Et je n'oserais pas entrer
   Tout ce qui se passe derrière

On parle
   Et je peux écouter

Mon sort était en jeu dans la pièce à côté

MIRACLE

HANGING head
        Eyelashes curled
Mouth silent
The lights go on
There is nothing there but a name
        Which has been forgotten
If the door opens
I won't dare go in
        Everything happens back there

They talk
        And I listen

My fate is at stake in the next room

Tout s'est éteint
Le vent passe en chantant
                Et les arbres frissonnent
Les animaux sont morts
Il n'y a plus personne
                    Regarde
Les étoiles ont cessé de briller
                La terre ne tourne plus
Une tête s'est inclinée
                Les cheveux balayant la nuit
Le dernier clocher resté debout
                Sonne minuit

A RINGING BELL

THE lights are all out
The wind passes singing
            And the trees shiver
The animals are dead
Nobody is left
                        Look
The stars have stopped sparkling
                The earth turns no more
A head nods
                The hair sweeps the night
The last steeple still standing
                Rings midnight

C'est bien l'automne qui revient
Va-t-on chanter
Mais plus personne
que moi
n'y tient
Je serai le dernier

Mais elle n'est pas si triste
qu'on l'avait dit
cette pâle saison
Un peu plus de mélancolie
Pour vous donner raison

La fumée interroge
Sera-ce lui ou toi
qui en ferez l'éloge
avant les premiers froids

Et moi j'attends
La dernière lumière
qui monte dans la nuit

Mais la terre descend
Et tout n'est pas fini
Une aile la supporte
Pendant tout ce temps
Avec toi j'irai à la fin du compte
Refermer la porte
S'il fait trop de vent

ONE WHO WAITS

It is indeed autumn that returns
Will someone sing
But nobody
except me
cares
I shall be the last

But she is not as sad
as has been said
this pale season
A little more sadness
To prove your point

The smoke asks
Will it be him or you
who will praise it
before the first frosts

And me I wait
For the last light
to rise in the night

But the earth descends
It's not all over
A wing supports it
All the time
I will go with you to the end of the line
To close the door
If it's too windy

JE TENAIS À TOUT

DANS les cloisons de l'air écoute un bruit de pas
Les oiseaux tournent sur ma tête
Leurs cercles ne resteront pas
Mais au fond de l'allée la porte s'est ouverte
On chante bas
Les gens qui passent
n'écoutent pas

Si vos yeux regardaient en l'air

On n'ira pas plus haut que les marches
du grenier ou du paradis
Le temps s'écaille
Dans la chambre où mon ombre a peu à peu grandi
La cloche appelle les passants
Ceux qui s'en vont et ceux qui rentrent
On voudrait ne pas entendre
Mais il faut bientôt repartir
On ne peut pas toujours dormir
Oublier l'heure qui passe
Connaître ce qui va venir
Un nom crié à toutes forces
Regarde sous tes fenêtres
Une figure inconnue qui n'a pas de corps
La rue déserte
La porte ouverte
Tous les trésors rêvés
Ma liberté aussi
Derrière moi sur le pavé
Une chaîne traîne sans bruit

I WANT EVERYTHING

In the partitions of air listen a sound of footsteps
Birds turn over my head
Their circles won't last
The gate is open at the end of the walk
Someone is singing low
The passersby
don't listen

If your eyes look upward

You will go no higher than the steps
of the attic or of paradise
Time flakes away
In the room where my shadow grows little by little
The bell calls the passersby
Those who go and those who return
You wish you couldn't hear it
You've got to go soon
You can't sleep all the time
To forget the passing hour
To know what's coming
A name cried out loud
Look under your windows
An unknown bodiless face
The deserted street
The open door
All the treasures you dreamed of
My liberty also
Behind me on the pavement
Drags a noiseless chain

CHEMIN TOURNANT

Il y a un terrible gris de poussière dans le temps
Un vent du sud avec de fortes ailes
Les échos sourds de l'eau dans le soir chavirant
Et dans la nuit mouillée qui jaillit du tournant
   des voix rugueuses qui se plaignent
Un goût de cendre sur la langue
Un bruit d'orgue dans les sentiers
Le navire du cœur qui tangue
Tous les désastres du métier

Quand les feux du désert s'éteignent un à un
Quand les yeux sont mouillés comme des brins d'herbe
Quand la rosée descend les pieds nus sur les feuilles
Le matin à peine levé
Il y a quelqu'un qui cherche
Une adresse perdue dans le chemin caché
Les astres dérouillés et les fleurs dégringolent
À travers les branches cassées
Et le ruisseau obscur essuieses lèvres molles à peine décollées
Quand le pas du marcheur sur le cadran qui compte
règle le mouvement et pousse l'horizon
Tous les cris sont passés tous les temps se rencontrent
Et moi je marche au ciel les yeux dans les rayons
Il y a du bruit pour rien et des noms dans ma tête
Des visages vivants
         Tout ce qui s'est passé au monde
  Et cette fête
       Où j'ai perdu mon temps

TURNING ROAD

Iᴛ is frightening grey dusty weather
A south wind on strong wings
Dull echoes of water in the capsizing evening
And in the soaking night spouting turning
    rough voices complaining
A taste of ashes on the tongue
The sound of an organ in the byways
The pitching ship of the heart
All the disasters of work

When the fires of the desert go out one by one
When the eyes drip like blades of grass
When the dew falls barefoot on the leaves
Morning hardly risen
Somebody seeks
A lost address on a lost road
The stars brighten the flowers tumble down
Across the broken branches
The dark brook wipes its soft scarce parted lips
When the steps of the walker on the counting dial
order the movement and crowd the horizon
All cries pass and all times meet
And me I walk to heaven my eyes in the rays
Noise about nothing and names in my head
Living faces
        Everything that has happened in the world
And this holiday
        Where I have lost my time

Iᴌ n'y a pas de trace
           au passage
                  la tête s'en va
Le courant d'air sur la pierre
           plus vite dans la rivière
                  Et toujours plus bas
Quand le bruit sourd qui résonne
           Que se lève l'homme
                  Et le jour qui passe tombe
                  au bord de la place
                  où l'autre mourra
Tous ceux qui sont là regardent
           ne comprennent pas
           Et les regards qui se lassent
                  s'usent
                  se détachent
           Les yeux glissent
                  vers un autre endroit
Au carrefour des six routes
           L'arrêt de nos pas
On irait plus loin sans doute
           Mais on n'ose pas

BEYOND

Not a footprint
        at the crossing
               the head goes off
Current of air on stone
        quicker in the river
           And always lower
When the dull noise resounds
        To arouse the man
        And the passing day falls
        beside the square
        where the other will die
Everybody there stares
        without understanding
    And the weary stares
            wear out
      fall off
The eyes slide
        toward another place
To the meeting of six roads
      Our steps halt
Maybe we should go further
      But we don't dare

Qu'on nous raconte cette histoire
Qu'on nous dise ce qu'il est devenu
Que personne autre que lui ne parle plus
Il rit
La rue est noire
La nuit vient doucement
Et l'esprit s'abandonne
À d'autres mouvements
Dans le fond à genoux sur le tas de pierres
Et les mains liées
Tous ceux qui pardonnent
Au cœur bourrelé
Ils sont encore tous là derrière
Les regards étoilés
Tous les noms confondus
Les rires étouffés
Les numéros perdus
Enfin le vent brutal les a tous dispersés
Et seul il s'en allait dans l'ombre sans écho
Il regardait le ciel le mur la terre et l'eau
L'histoire   le remords
Tout était oublié
Ce n'était plus du tout le même
Au coin   quand il s'est retourné

HOW TO CHANGE

LET somebody tell the story
        Let somebody say what happened to him
Let nobody else talk anymore
        He laughs
The street is black
Night comes softly
                And the spirit abandons itself
                To other movements
At the bottom kneeling on a heap of stones
                With hands bound
                All those who forgive
                The tortured heart
They are all still back there
                Starry-eyed
                All the names confused
                The laughs stifled
                The numbers lost
At last the brutal wind scatters them all
And he goes alone into echoless shadow
He has seen heaven wall earth water
History   remorse
            It's all forgotten
It's not the same at all anymore
At the corner   when he turns around

Un entonnoir immense où se tordait la nuit
    Des lambeaux s'échappaient par moments
Des lueurs qui allaient s'éteindre bien plus loin
     Tout était pâle
  L'aube
  Le soleil naissant
  Une boule à peine ronde
  Le reflet du monde
  Sur l'écran
Une ligne horizontale se tendait
    L'air se mettait à vibrer
    Il fallait attendre
Les voix qui revenaient de loin
    Rappelaient ta vie en arrière
Mais le chemin qu'il aurait fallu refaire était trop long
Les voix familières trop tristes
Les yeux qui te regardent sont sinistres
   On ne peut plus avancer
Toutes les portes sont fermées
Derrière quelqu'un écoute plaqué contre le mur
   Et le rideau qui tremble
      retombe
Il te ressemble
   Le centre se déplace
Les parois inclinées rendent le ciel plus grand
   L'ombre déborde
   La tête se penchait

GALLERIES

Night twists in an immense funnel
       Tatters fall off every few minutes
From the lights going out in the distance
           All pale
   Dawn
   Newborn sun
   A ball hardly round
   The reflection of the world
   On the screen
A horizontal line stretches out
       The air starts to throb
       You had to wait
The voices come back from far off
      Calling back your life
But the road back is too long
The familiar voices too sad
Sinister eyes watch you
      You can't go on
All the doors are shut
Behind them somebody is listening flattened against the wall
    And the curtain trembles
            drops again
He resembles you
     The center shifts
Inclined walls make the sky bigger
    The shadow overflows
    The head nods

C'est celle d'un malade
                    Et la seule qui existait
                    Une étoile se déclouait
          Tout près
La main lentement se soulève
Le front plissé a dissipé son rêve
Et tout ce qui derrière était passé
                    Une seule fois
                    dans le temps qui s'amasse
On ne regarde pas
               C'est à recommencer
Mais quand pourra-t-on revenir
Au moment où tout peut finir
               La vie entière est en jeu
Constamment
Nous passons à côté du vide élégamment
                    sans tomber
Mais parfois quelque chose en nous fait tout trembler
Et le monde n'existe plus
               Nos yeux se trompent
L'on n'entend plus le même son
La même voix
C'est derrière l'univers soi-même que l'on voit
               Une silhouette qui danse
La série de portraits qui ne rappellent rien
               De ceux que l'on ne connaît pas
Ce sont des gens qui vous regardent
               Des cadres éclatants les gardent

It's a sick man's
              And the only one alive
              A star comes unnailed
        Very near
The hand lifts slowly
The wrinkled brow dissipates its dream
And everything that happened behind it
              Only once
              in gathering time
You don't look
              It's got to start again
But when can we return
To the moment when it all can end
              Our whole life is at stake
Constantly
We pass elegantly along the void
                    and don't fall
But sometimes something in us makes everything
    tremble
And the world ceases
              Our eyes are tricked
You don't hear the same sound anymore
The same voice
Behind the universe itself you can see
        A dancing silhouette
The series of portraits recalls nothing
        Of those you never knew
These people who stare at you
        Shiny frames preserve them

Au milieu de ces visages immobiles
Le seul qui soit vivant
                    Paraît le plus tranquille
Il part pour ne plus revenir
Dans la salle où les murs se sont mis à sourire
Il n'y a plus que la nuit qui monte pour sortir
        Un pas résonnant sur la dalle
Il fait froid
Ton regard levé vers les étoiles

In the midst of those immobile faces
The only one alive
                    Seems the calmest
He leaves never to return
To the room where the walls begin to smile
Nothing anymore but night rising to leave
        A footstep echoing on the flagstone
It grows cold
Your eyes lift to the stars

Petite poitrine
   O
nuages
       Dans l'étang où elle se noya
       L'hiver ne souffle plus
Et
loin de son bord
Il passe ayant remis son pardessus
Dans la vitrine tout le monde la regarde
Elle est morte et sourit à ces gens
           qui ne savent que douter
Sa petite poitrine a l'air de remuer
Avec vos lèvres vous soufflez dessus
Et ses yeux se ferment en vous regardant
Ces messieurs habillés de noir
Ont les yeux brillants de malice
Une petite femme que j'ai beaucoup connue
La misère passe avec le vent
et balaie le boulevard
       Elle avait de bien jolies jambes
       Elle dansait elle riait
Et maintenant que va-t-elle devenir
Tournant la tête
elle demandait qu'on la laissât dormir

FLOWER MARKET

LITTLE breast
  O
clouds
      In the pond where she drowned herself
      Winter blows no more
And
far from its shore
He puts on his overcoat and goes away
Everybody stares at her in the showcase
She is dead and smiles at the people
        who don't know what to think
Her little breast seems to stir
When you blow on it with your lips
And her eyes close as they watch you
These gentlemen dressed in black
Have eyes brilliant with malice
A little woman I once knew well
Misery goes with the wind
sweeping the boulevard
        She had very pretty legs
        She danced and laughed
And now what will become of her
She turns her head
and asks to be left asleep

SPECTACLE DES YEUX

Les têtes qui dépassaient la ligne sont tombées
Tout le monde crie aux fenêtres
D'autres sont aussi dans la rue
Au milieu du bruit et des rires
Il y a des animaux qu'on n'avait jamais vus
Les passants familiers
Et les visages d'or
Les voix sur les sentiers
Et les accents plus forts
Puis vers midi le soleil les clairons
Les hommes plus joyeux qui se mettent à rire
Les maisons qui ouvrent leurs yeux
Les seuils s'accueillent d'un sourire
Quand le cortège flotte dans la poussière
L'enfant aux yeux brûlés d'étonnement
Contre la femme en tablier bleu
L'enfant blond et l'ange peureux
Devant ces gens venus d'ailleurs
qui ne ressemblent pas à ceux que l'on connaît
Avec qui l'on voudrait partir
Étrangers merveilleux qui passent sans mourir
Le soir rallume ses lumières
Le spectacle dresse ses feux
La danseuse enflammée sort du portemanteau
Les maillots gonflés se raniment

SPECTACLE FOR THE EYES

THE heads that got out of line have fallen
Everybody yells out the windows
Others are also in the street
In the middle of noise and laughter
There are animals you have never seen
Familiar passersby
Golden faces
Voices on the paths
Broad accents
Then about noon the sun the trumpets
Men so happy they start to laugh
Houses opening their eyes
The doorsills smile with welcome
When the parade floats in dust
A child with eyes burning with astonishment
Against the wife with a blue apron
The blond child and the angel
Timid before all these people come together
like nobody they ever knew
Whom they'd like to go away with
Marvelous deathless foreigners who go by
The evening lights its lamps again
The show sets up its flares
The blazing dancer comes out of her suitcase
The swollen tights come to life

La fortune court sur le corps
La lune roule dans la piste
On saute à travers ce décor
Pendant que l'ombre basse équivoque du cirque
Tourne avec les clameurs
Et que l'enfant rêveur aux songes magnifiques
Pleure sur sa laideur

The one-wheeled bicycle runs on the frame
The spotlight rolls in the track
They jump through the scenery
While the equivocal deep shadow of the circus
Revolves with the racket
And the child dreamer of magnificent dreams
Weeps for his own ugliness

SUR LA POINTE DES PIEDS

Il n'y a plus rien qui reste
          entre mes dix doigts
Une ombre qui s'efface
        Au centre
          un bruit de pas
Il faut étouffer la voix qui monte trop
Celle qui gémissait et qui ne mourait pas
Celle qui allait plus vite
C'est vous qui arrêtiez ce magnifique élan
          L'espoir et mon orgueil
            qui passaient dans le vent
Les feuilles sont tombées
          pendant que les oiseaux comptaient
              les gouttes d'eau
Les lampes s'éteignaient derrière les rideaux
Il ne faut pas aller trop vite
Crainte de tout casser en faisant trop de bruit

ON TIPTOE

Nothing stays anymore
        between my ten fingers
A vanishing shadow
      At the center
      a footstep
Choke off the voice that rises too high
That moaned and wouldn't die
That went too fast
It was you who put a stop to this magnificent ardor
     Hope and my pride
       have passed on the wind
The leaves fell
      while the birds were counting
          the drops of water
The lamps went out behind the curtains
Not so fast
Be careful you'll break everything with so much noise

PERSPECTIVE

La même voiture
M'a-t-elle emporté
                    Je vois d'où tu viens
                    Tu tournes la tête

Minuit
Sur la lune
Finit de sonner
                    Au coin de la rue
                    Tout est retourné

J'ai vu sa figure
Et même ses mains
                    La dernière étoile
                    Est dans le jardin

Comme la première
On pense à demain
                    Mais où seront-ils
                    Morts sans y penser
Quand le mur s'efface
                    Le ciel va tomber

PERSPECTIVE

Dɪᴅ the same
Car carry me away
                    I see where you came from
                    You turn your head
Midnight
On the moon
Just struck
                    At the street corner
                    Everything is turned around
I saw her face
Even her hands
                    The last star
                    Is in the garden
Just like the first
Think of tomorrow
                    Where will they be
                    The thoughtless dead
When the wall vanishes
                    The sky will fall

LE MONDE DEVANT MOI

QUELQUE temps passé
La nuit claire
Un nouveau soleil s'est levé
Le lendemain
Un vieillard à genoux tendait les mains
Les animaux couraient tout le long du chemin

Je me suis assis
J'ai rêvé
Une fenêtre s'ouvre sur ma tête
Il n'y a personne dedans
Un homme passe derrière la haie

La campagne où chante un seul oiseau
Quelqu'un a peur
Et l'on s'amuse
Là-bas entre deux petits enfants
La joie
Toi contre moi
La pluie efface les larmes

On ne peut pas marcher dans le sentier étroit
On rentre du même côté
Mais il y a une barrière
Quelque chose vient de tomber
Là-bas derrière

Une ombre plus grande que lui-même
fait le tour de la terre
Et moi je suis resté assis sans oser regarder

THE WORLD BEFORE ME

Some time ago
Clear night
New sunrise
Next day
An old man on his knees holds out his hands
Animals ran all along the road

I sit me down
I have dreamed
A window opens on my head
Nobody home
A man goes by behind the hedge

The countryside where a single bird sings
Somebody is afraid
Somebody is amused
Down there between two little children
Joy
You against me
Rain washes away tears

You can't walk the narrow path
You go back the same way
There is a gate
Something just fell
Down behind there

His shadow bigger than himself
goes around the earth
And me I just sit there and don't dare look

Une petit lumière
Tu vois une petite lumière descendre sur ton ventre
    pour t'éclairer
—Une femme s'étire comme une fusée—
Au coin là-bas une ombre lit
Ses pieds libres sont trop jolis

Court-circuit au cœur
Une panne au moteur
Quel aimant me soutient
Mes yeux et mon amour se trompent de chemin

Un rien
Un feu que l'on rallume et qui s'éteint
J'ai assez du vent
J'ai assez du ciel
Au fond tout ce qu'on voit est artificiel
Même ta bouche
Pourtant j'ai chaud là où ta main me touche
La porte est ouverte et je n'entre pas
Je vois ton visage et je n'y crois pas
Tu es pâle
Un soir qu'on était triste on a pleuré sur une malle
Là-bas des hommes riaient
Des enfants presque nus parfois se promenaient
L'eau était claire
Un fil de cuivre rouge y conduit la lumière
Le soleil et ton cœur sont de même matière

CENTRAL HEATING

A little light
Look a little light descends on your belly and
  lights you up
—A woman stretches herself like a rocket—
Over there in the corner a shadow reads
Her bare feet are too pretty

Short circuit in the heart
Breakdown in the motor
What magnet holds me up
My eyes and love have lost their way

A nothing
A fire we keep lighting which keeps going out
I've had wind
I've had sky
At bottom everything we see is artificial
Even your mouth
Yet I get hot where your hand touches me
The door is open and I don't go in
I see your face and I don't believe it
You're pale
One night we were sad and wept on our trunk
Men laughed down there
Children strolled around almost naked
The water was clear
Copper wire conducts the light
The sun and your heart are made of the same material

Une minute à peine
        Et je suis revenu
De tout ce qui passait je n'ai rien retenu
Un point
     Le ciel grandi
         Et au dernier moment
La lanterne qui passe
       Le pas que l'on entend
   Quelqu'un s'arrête entre tout ce qui marche
On laisse aller le monde
       Et ce qu'il y a dedans
Les lumières qui dansent
      Et l'ombre qui s'étend
Il y a plus d'espace
        En regardant devant
Une cage où bondit un animal vivant
La poitrine et les bras faisaient le même geste
Une femme riait
      En renversant la tête
Et celui qui venait nous avait confondus
Nous étions tous les trois sans nous connaître
Et nous formions déjà
      Un monde plein d'espoir

MEMORY

Just a minute
　　　And I am back
Of everything that's gone I have kept nothing
A point
　　　The wide sky
　　　　　　And at the last moment
The lantern goes by
　　　　　　The step you hear
　Somebody stops and everything else goes on
You let the world go
　　　　　　And what is inside
Dancing lights
　　　　　　Outstretched shadows
There is still space
　　　　　　Looking ahead
A cage where a live animal leaps
Breast and arms make the same motion
A woman was laughing
　　　　　　With her head thrown back
And the man who came mistook us
We didn't know each other all three of us
And yet we formed
　　　　　　A world full of hope

NATURE MORTE - PORTRAIT

Le nil le calendrier et la blague à tabac
Nature
Comme doit être la peinture
Morte
Et la littérature
Une tête sans chevelure
Des yeux en trait
Une virgule
Un nez plat un méplat
Au front
Mon portrait
Mon cœur bat
Et c'est la pendule
Dans la glace je suis en pied
Ma tête fume

STILL LIFE - PORTRAIT

CIGARETTE papers datebook and tobacco pouch
Life
Ought to be like painting
Still
And literature
A hairless head
Eyes straight
Comma
A flat nose a plane
On the forehead
My portrait
My heart beats
It's an alarm clock
In the mirror I'm full length
My head smokes

L'HOMME SACRIFIÉ

Il n'y a que le bleu des taches dans ce coin de drap
Des souvenirs des sourires au casier
Une tête et des épines sur la couronne des bras
Les épaules remuent
Enfin le moulin bouge
Et la montagne au fil d'airain
Glisse autour du monde
Quelque part où les portes s'ouvrent
Sur les numéros en ordre
Assemblés à leur nom
Par rang de taille
On appelle
Et sur toute la foule
Il pleut des éclats de verre
Ou de rosée
L'humidité des plages gagne le milieu le plus aride
    du sol
Et sous les trépidations de la danse les immeubles
Gâtés par le soleil et la fraîcheur s'effritent
Puis des feuilles naissant au bout des doigts
    des jeunes filles
Les yeux s'ouvrent sous la mousse
Et les pieds écrasant parfois les paupières
Alors les rideaux s'abaissent encore plus bas
La tête tourne et se cache dans le creux des bras
Et les souvenirs s'émeuvent
La nuit qui s'en va

SACRIFIED MAN

NOTHING but blue spots in the corner of a sheet
Memories of smiles filed away
A head and thorns on a crown of arms
Heaving shoulders
At last the mill moves
And the mountain of brass wire
Slides around the world
Somewhere doors open
On ordered numbers
Gathered by name
By height
Rollcall
Over the whole mob
Rain splinters of glass
Or dew
The dampness of the shores penetrates to the middle
    of the driest soil
And beneath their shivering dance the houses
Rotted by sun and chill wear away
Then leaves are born from young girls' fingertips
Eyes open under moss
Now and then feet crush eyelids
Then curtains are drawn still lower
The head turns and hides in the hollow of the arms
Memories stir
Night goes

Pour éviter l'écueil qui se tient en arrière
Qui me suit
Qui attend le pas définitif
Pour éviter de jamais revenir en arrière
Sur le flanc de l'amour qui glisse sans mourir
Cet amour qui se dégage mal de tes viscères
Ces regards qui n'ont plus ni rime ni raison
Et ce portrait de toi que je voudrais refaire
Tendre cruel vivant dans l'ombre sans passion
Ce regard qui se perd dans la nuit jalouse
Ce regard plein des pointes de feu de la jalousie
Dans la robe du soir dont se pare la terre
Au moment où tu sors

Loin dans le désespoir
J'aurai le visage enfoui dans la glace
Le cœur percé des mille feux du souvenir
L'écueil de l'avenir et la mort en arrière
Et ton sourire trop léger
Une barrière
De toi à moi
Les paroles libres
Les gestes retenus
Des mains ailées qui avançaient pour tout ouvrir
Alors dans la trame serrée livide se découvre
La blessure inouïe dont je voudrais guérir

X

To escape the danger behind me
That follows me
That waits the definitive step
To shun turning back
Across the flank of love that slips deathless
This love that disengages painfully from your bowels
Those looks that no longer have rhyme or reason
And your portrait I want to do over
Tender cruel living in passionless shadow
Your gaze lost in jealous night
Your gaze full of jealousy's points of fire
Dressed in the evening gown the earth puts on
As soon as you go out

Far in hopelessness
My face will be buried in ice
Dry heart stabbed with memory's thousand fires
The reef of the future and death behind me
And your too faint smile
A barrier
Between you and me
Free words
Clinging gestures
Winged hands advanced to open everything
Then in the tight livid warp is revealed
The unheard of wound I want to cure

LES BATTEMENTS DU CŒUR

On remettra peut-être enfin la mécanique en marche
   sous les palmes
Sur la claire cimaise où l'ombre tourne mal
À l'aube des parties décidées loin du port
Quand les idées sans lest prennent le large
Dans l'immense rainure où s'évacue la soif
Où le sang trop léger reconstitue ses vagues
Quand la houle pousse à grands coups d'épaule
   sur le bord
Le chant des matelots haletant la cadence

On pourrait à la rigueur compter les mots
Aligner tous les traits cassés de ces visages
Au front du ciel les rides trop creusées par les efforts
Et les douleurs durement adaptées à la forme des hommes
Il faut voir ces statues de liège sur les flots
Ces formes déguisées qui s'accablent dans l'ombre
Quand l'esprit clairvoyant dans l'éclair d'un défaut
Aperçoit l'avenir implacable sur les arêtes de la tombe

Qui penserait à revenir alors par un autre chemin
Qui oserait gravir les marches du calvaire
Une ligne de trop déclasse mon tourment
Avec un regard plus perfide on perd le cœur
   de l'adversaire
Plus une larme dans le mien
Plus un geste précis sur l'écran troublé du mystère
Rien que des signes noirs sur les routes sans fin
Et tout le temps perdu dans les fausses carrières

HEART BEATS

MAYBE at last they'll start up the machines
   under the palms
On the bright picture molding where the shadow turns wrong
In the dawn of games won far from port
When notions without ballast take off
Into the immense channel where thirst empties
Where the slight blood reconstitutes its waves
When the surge shoves with great pushes of its shoulders
   against the shore
The sailors' song panting its cadence

If you had to you could count the words
Line up all the broken features of those faces
The wrinkles too deeply creased by effort on the sky's forehead
And sorrows severely formed to the shape of men
You ought to see those cork statues on the billows
Those disguised forms crushed in the shadows
When the clairvoyant spirit in the flash of a fault
Perceives the implacable future on the rooftree of the tomb

Who would think he could go back then by another road
Who would dare climb the stages of the Way of the Cross
One line too many degrades my torment
You can destroy the adversary's heart with a still more
   perfidious look
No longer any tear in mine
No longer any precise action on the screen troubled with mystery
Nothing but black signs along endless roads
And all the time lost on false courses

Mais parfois la joie ouvre ses branches d'or au soleil
 caressant
L'amour épanoui depuis les premiers murmures
 du jour se dépouille de ses pétales
Contre l'orgueil meurtri par la rudesse de tes mains
Les bras serrant plus fort ton cou
À chaque soubresaut de mon terrible caractère
Ces bras qui seront désormais la rugueuse ceinture
 de tes reins
Dont tu ne pourras te défaire
La force sans répit qui tressera nos liens
Sous le mal que tu peux me faire

But now and then joy opens golden branches to the
  caressing sun
Love blooming since the first murmurs of day sheds its
  petals
Against pride hurt by the roughness of your hands
My arms clinging more tightly to your neck
At each spasm of my terrible character
Those arms which henceforth will be the wrinkled
  girdle of your thighs
Which you will never be able to put off
The relentless force which braids our bonds
Under the evil you can do to me

Sous l'arc des nuages durcis
Au bruit des voix qui s'abandonnent
Sur les trottoirs blancs et les rails
À travers les branches du temps
J'ai regardé passer ton ombre
Seule entre les signes obscurs
Les traits de lumière mouvante
Transparente au reflet des fausses devantures
Et elle allait et elle allait
Jamais tu n'as marché si vite
Je me rappelais ta figure
Mais elle était beaucoup moins grande
Et puis j'ai regardé ailleurs
Mais pour te retrouver encore
Dans les échos de jour roulant dans ma mémoire

Des fils de souvenirs s'accrochent dans les branches
Des feuilles dans l'air bleu planent à contre vent
Un ruisseau de sang clair se glisse sous la pierre
Les larmes et la pluie sur le même buvard
Puis tout se mêle au choc dans l'ouate plus épaisse
Dans l'écheveau du sort le cœur perd son chemin
Toujours le même qui s'arrête
Toujours le même qui revient

Le soleil s'éteignait
Je regardais plus loin
Les traces de tes pas brodaient d'or la poussière
Et tout ce qui n'était pas là
Dans les flammes du soir qui dévorent la terre

RAINBOW

Under the arch of hard clouds
To the noise of abandoned voices
On the white sidewalks and rails
Across the branches of time
I have watched your shadow go by
Alone between obscure signs
Shafts of moving light
Transparent in the reflections of false store windows
And she went on and she went on
You never walked so quickly
I recalled your face
But it was not so big
And then I looked around
To find you again
In the echoes of the day rolling in my memory

Threads of memories cling to the branches
Leaves glide down through blue air against the wind
A stream of bright blood slides under the stones
Tears and rain on the same blotter
Then it's all mixed up in shock in the thickest wadding
The heart loses its way in the tangles of fate
Always the same one stops
Always the same one returns

The sun went out
I looked further
Your footprints embroidered the dust with gold
And everything that wasn't there
In the flames of evening devouring the earth

FIGURE délayée dans l'eau
Dans le silence
Trop de poids sur la gorge
Trop d'eau dans le bocal
Trop d'ombre renversée
Trop de sang sur la rampe
Il n'est jamais fini
Ce rêve de cristal

FACE diluted in water
In silence
Too much weight on the breast
Too much water in the pitcher
Too much darkness spilled
Too much blood on the stair
It will never end
This crystal dream

OUTRE MESURE

Le monde est ma prison
Si je suis loin de ce que j'aime
Vous n'êtes pas trop loin barreaux de l'horizon
L'amour la liberté dans le ciel trop vide
Sur la terre gercée de douleurs
Un visage éclaire et réchauffe les choses dures
Qui faisaient partie de la mort
A partir de cette figure
De ces gestes de cette voix
Ce n'est que moi-même qui parle
Mon cœur qui résonne et qui bat
Un écran de feu abat-jour tendre
Entre les murs familiers de la nuit
Cercle enchanté des fausses solitudes
Faisceaux de reflets lumineux
Regrets
Tous ces débris du temps crépitent au foyer
Encore un plan qui se déchire
Un acte qui manque à l'appel
Il reste peu de chose à prendre
Dans un homme qui va mourir

OUT OF PROPORTION

THE world is my prison
If I am far from what I love
You are not too far barriers of the horizon
Love and liberty in a sky too empty
On the earth chapped with sorrow
A face shines forth and warms the hard things
That were a part of death
Starting from that face
From those acts from that voice
It is only myself speaking
My heart resounding and beating
A screen of fire a tender shutter
Between the familiar walls of night
Enchanted circle of false solitudes
Bundles of luminous reflections
Regrets
All the debris of time crackles on the hearth
Another plan torn up
Another act missed its cue
There are few things left to take
From a dying man

Lève-toi carcasse et marche
Rien de neuf sous le soleil jaune
Le der des der des louis d'or
La lumière qui se détache
sous les pellicules du temps
La serrure au cœur qui éclate
Un fil de soie
Un fil de plomb
Un fil de sang
Après ces vagues de silence
Ces signes d'amour au crin noir
Le ciel plus lisse que ton œil
Le cou tordu d'orgueil
Ma vie dans la coulisse
D'où je vois onduler les moissons de la mort
Toutes ces mains avides qui pétrissent des boules
    de fumée
Plus lourdes que les piliers de l'univers
Têtes vides
Cœurs nus
Mains parfumées
Tentacules des singes qui visent les nuées
Dans les rides de ces grimaces
Une ligne droite se tend
Un nerf se tord
La mer repue
L'amour
L'amer sourire de la mort

LIVE FLESH

RISE up carcass and walk
Nothing new under the yellow sun
The very last of the very last gold pieces
The light which detaches itself
under the films of time
The lock of the bursting heart
A silk thread
A lead wire
A trickle of blood
After waves of silence
These signs of love's black pelt
Heaven slippery as your eye
The neck wrenched with pride
My life in the wings
Where I can watch the harvests of death undulate
All these avid hands kneading balls of smoke
Heavier than the pillars of the universe
Empty heads
Naked hearts
Perfumed hands
Monkey tentacles aiming at the clouds
In the wrinkles of those grimaces
A straight line bends
A nerve twists
The sated sea
Love
Death's bitter smile

ET MAINTENANT

Pas de source ce soir
Pas de fruits sous les feuilles
L'orage s'est calmé trop tard
L'amour ni la raison ne montent à l'oreille
Les tranches détachées du cœur dans les allées
Tout ce que le matin redore
Au détour de la nuit féroce et tourmentée
Comme le vent qui frotte et secoue
Et rit
Le vent d'hier gonflé sur l'aire
Vers midi
Bulles d'air prisonnier
Chansons détruites
Ou bien encore le sel de la passion sourde
qui vous dévore
Qui brûle le creux de vos mains
Qui perce les plans du soleil
La plaie sèche et noire d'orgueil
Dans la lumière éblouissante de la bouche
Sous la cendre un chagrin qui veille
Un frisson de cristal
Un timbre mal posé qui tremble
Et se recueille
Étouffé par la sève ardente des tourments
Du sang chargé des âcretés de la savane
Un nuage sur l'œil

AND NOW

No spring this evening
No fruits under the leaves
The storm is calmed too late
Neither love nor reason rises to the ear
Detached slices of heart along the walks
Everything morning regilds
In the turning of the fierce and tormented night
Like the wind that rubs and jolts
And laughs
The wind of yesterday swollen in volume
Towards noon
Captive bubbles of air
Destroyed songs
Or still better the salt of deaf passion
which devours you
Which burns the hollow of your hands
Which stabs the planes of sunlight
The wound dry and black with pride
In the mouth's dazzling light
Under the ashes an anger watches
A shiver of crystal
A misplaced stamp trembles
And collects itself
Choked by the burning sap of tortures
Of blood charged with the acridity of the savannah
A cloud on the eye

Un front comme le ciel sur les ravins vertigineux
    de la figure
Dans un cadre de sable blanc
La trame enchevêtrée reprise au sens de l'heure
Les pointes de feu du désir
Les cicatrices de la haine
Et rien pour retenir la vie
Rien pour couper le fil qui se dévide
Alors tous les échos perdus dans la rumeur
Les voix éclaboussées sur la mousse des murs
Les traits de la passion tordus dans les décombres
Dans le filet vers les lueurs lointaines
Et ces mains suspendues au fil de l'horizon
Tant de signes d'amour
Tant d'ailes dans les rampes
Du sommet de la neige aux flocons de la mer
Quand l'air s'embrouille dans les branches
Dans la forme des mains
Dans la source des poches
Il y a de l'or et de l'argent
Il y a de l'esprit dans la manche
Quand la couleur coule à pleins bords
Le cœur va plus loin que les yeux
La flamme renaît de la cendre
Entre le fil qui coule et le trait lumineux
les mots n'ont plus de sens
D'ailleurs on n'a plus besoin des mots pour se comprendre
Une clarté remue au coin le plus creux de la chambre
Une tête lourde s'endort

A forehead like heaven over the vertiginous ravines
    of the face
In a frame of white sand
The tangled warp reweaves the meaning of the hour
The points of fire of desire
The scars of hate
And nothing to keep life
Nothing to cut the reeled in thread
So all the echoes are lost in noise
The voices spattered on the mossy walls
The lines of passion twisted in rubble
In the thread towards the distant glimmer
And these hands hung from the line of the horizon
So many signs of love
So many wings in the stairways
From the summit of snow to the flakes of the sea
When the air is confused in the branches
In the form of hands
In the source of pockets
There's gold and silver
There's a soul up the sleeve
When color flows freely
The heart goes further than the eyes
Flame is reborn from the ashes
Between the flowing thread and the luminous line
words become senseless
Besides there's no more need of words to understand
Clarity stirs in the hollowest corner of the room
A heavy head drowses

Au pli de l'abat-jour la pointe d'une aile s'enfonce
C'est le vent qui bat tous les records
De ses vagues pressées à l'écluse des portes
L'espace devient noir
La fenêtre est bouchée
Le cœur est à peu près éteint
Les mains sont sans abri
Tous les arbres couchés
Il n'y a plus que quelques mots confus
    dans les derniers remous de la poitrine
Le piège est détendu
La rampe des rêves s'allume
Mémoire délivrée
Chagrins perdus dans l'air
Frontières dépassées
Tous les fils dénoués au delà des saisons reprennent
    leur tour et leur ton sur le fond sombre du silence

Through a fold in the windowshade a wing tip is thrust
It's the wind which beats all records
From its thronging waves to the lock of its gates
Space becomes black
The window shut up
The heart a little more extinguished
The hands without shelter
All the trees put to bed
Only some confused words in the last eddy of the breast
The trap sprung
The stairs of dream lit up
Memory set free
Sorrow lost in air
Escaped frontiers
All threads untangled beyond all seasons learning
    their turn and tone under the dark depth of silence

INDEX of Titles and First Lines

English